The Poor Broken Poet

THE POOR BROKEN POET

BY A. AMAR

A. Amar
poorbrokenpoet@gmail.com

ISBN 978-1-71654-877-2

Printed in the United States of America

First Printing, 2020

Cover Art: Anja Rösgen (Mrs. White Photoart)

To a faceless woman with many faces.

Your rotten soul smells like poetry.

Contents

I sit skinless   1
I never wanted to write   3
Weaving the strands   5

Chapter One: Elation   7
Chapter Two: Shock   37
Chapter Three: Anger   47
Chapter Four: Bargaining   85
Chapter Five: Depression   107
Chapter Six: Acceptance   169

Acknowledgements   197

THE POOR BROKEN POET

I sit skinless,
raw with emotion.
The love she vacated
left a bittersweet corpse.
I use the bones to cut the canvas,
the tears as war paint,
and the remains to write the eulogy.

I never wanted to write.

But love has held
me so closely
that it squeezed
out letters.

Weaving the strands
of memories left
from lost unions,

they blend
into a mosaic
that I call *her*.

I can feel the heartbeat
from the chest
that used to press
against me.

A synchronicity
that endlessly echoes
what we shared.

A soft glow that
surrounded her face
when we made love.

I have tasted heaven.

This pattern of thoughts
certainly borders obsession.

But I spoke with God
when I held her attention.

Chapter One

Elation

Beautiful and naïve,
she approaches.
I sit in a slump
with sunken eye sockets.

She flashes
an adorable glimmer
of hope.

Her optimist's mind
believes she is here
to save mine.

She stares up
at the monster inside me
with confidence.
Behind me
lie a pile of carcasses.

"Poor thing,"
we both thought.

Baby girl,
my inner child
is an arsonist,
and I'm still burning bridges.

My spirit animal
is a two-horned minotaur
that tramples well-wishes.

I appreciate the sentiment,
but please don't pick the locks
in this prison.

My tormented soul
hasn't finished its sentence.

Something as subtle
as the way she blinks
floods the corridors
of my intrigue.

The beautiful contrast
of her skin
as it connects to lips
the same color of rose hips.

I stare at her changing expressions
to melt permanence
into my later recollections.

I try to hold her hand
long enough to remove
any possibility
of disconnection.

She wants to know what I want,
but just looking at her
is too much to absorb
all at once.

She does this thing with her nose
that makes the strange-looking
thing in my underpants grow.

Her sighs of annoyance
are the wind that Cupid's arrows
are carried across.

Her biological traits
are just the cherry on top.
I like her sense of style
and the way she wears her heart.

The world looks at her like meat,
but I look at her as art.

As the wind flowed with her hair,

the strands spelled out meaning
like perfect letters in cursive.

They flew in every direction
that my emotions could conceive
as they moved with the leaves
of surrounding trees.

I couldn't keep up with all
that was happening.

The ends seemed to point to the places
I'd never known, and I remained stuck
as they reached into my soul.

They were her connection to every *thing*
and every *where*.

And all I cared to do was stare
as the wind flowed with her hair.

No one else exists.

I saw her
and lost my
peripheral vision.

She is
the sort
of beauty
they speak of
in stories.

Written with
the blood
of dead poets.

And I would hurt
them all again
if it meant
I'd get to find you
in the end.

She interlocks our fingers
and pulls me from a self-sentence
of solitary confinement.

She is brave to proceed
while aware of the failure
of each one who's tried it.

We both know my ego
is out of control,
but she swears my soul
is salvageable.

These rough palms
have pressed my eyes black
more times than I can account for.

I am afraid of zombies,
but all they fear is love.

I've bounced off
too many rubber souls,
and I've had enough.

My gloves are tired,
and there is no one left to fight.

I have tried the others on,
and they still don't fit right.

My mind is the enemy,
but my heart will love you indefinitely.

Please stay for a while,
as long as you know
that I'll run you off eventually.

I have seen love
within the glow
of a beautiful sunset,

in the shine
of the moonlight,
and in the glimmer
of a teardrop.

I seek salvation
from mortality
in a connection
that defines purpose,

in a mirror that reflects
everything beneath the surface.

Do not tell me
that love is blind,

for within its promiscuity,
there is only one
who knows my name.

I have touched enough flesh
to know what it's like.

I only want to penetrate
the part of you
that doesn't die.

There is nothing more naked
than what is in your eyes.

You wear that skin
like a translucent painting,
but there are teeth behind that smile.
And beyond that is a black hole
where your true feelings gather.
These are the parts of you
I'd prefer to know.

She saw my sad soul
and carved a hole
through its wall.

Her delicate hands
reached inside
and removed
what was meant to be broken.

She carefully stitched
the wound with a kiss
from the softest lips
ever placed on this chest.

She collapses
the dark skies
and brings the heavens
beneath my feet.

I study love.
Everything else
becomes obsolete.

Please remember
that Cupid's arrows
have barbed ends.

For as soft
as those lips must be,
they glisten with the danger
of a deadly reality.

I walk past delicately,
terrified of your ability
to swiftly liquefy
my crumbling sanity.

I admire the beauty
of your feathers
and the intricacies
of your inner workings.

The power of the those
perfectly painted talons
could crush my core
and drop me from
a sky of hope.

I'm already broken
on this desolate land,

a man with hammers for hands
who only wishes to caress
your soft sand.

I wasn't expecting
to make you mine:
I was only doing research
on different ways to die.

A lost pebble
sits battered on the never-ending
shoreline of a forgotten beach.

An empty shell
lies futureless, displaying the lines
of the glorious years it knew
before the end.

Birds follow the lead
of their homeless leader.

Patches of dirt
stain the landscapes of green.

Dead branches
lean against the mismatched limbs
of aging trees.

And somehow
you still see the beauty
in the ugly parts of me.

I press my ear
against her shell
to hear the peaceful sea.

I can feel her heartbeat
and the gentle creak
of her bones as her hands
caress my hair.

There's a war going on outside
which they all run towards,

but this could be
my final resting place.

I rub the grooves
of my fingerprints
across the pores
of her skin.

Goosebumps spread
like gentle ripples
from the center
of the ocean.

There is a beauty within the paradox in which man exists:
a universe of capability, a profound depth of thought,
feelings so immense they expand beyond the cosmos,
a boundless potential contained within a fragile,
ever-perishing, decaying shell.

I may not
have much,

but lend me
a drop of ink,

and I will paint
you the universe.

She reminds me to look
at the palette's spectrum
before I reach my findings,
but she doesn't know
I'm a colorblind artist.

The earth's tears
have oxidized
the silver lining,
and all that I see is the tarnish.

She thinks it's cute
when the dark hues
of my personality
bleed through.

They say the devil
has cloven hooves,
and I'm fond of the one
with hands of a fawn.

I gently ran my fingers
through her hair
to feel the texture
of her crown,
careful not to pierce
that thin layer of water
one breaks before they drown.

Perfect black strands
must be the missing waves
from the dead sea
of my relationships.

She suggests
a different topic,
but all my views
are misanthropic.

I want to lose
the color in my hair
before my eyes no longer see
the luminosity of your presence,

to touch your skin continuously
while I still own hands,

and to lose the life from this body
before I begin the journey
to find you again.

The worms
can wait.

I would
be happy
to slowly
rot with you.

She deserved
more than his
world could offer.

So he handed her
words in the shape
of gemstones.

And with those
three words
she gave me,
I will write
forever.

Each day I wake
next to you
will always be
the happy ending.

There is nothing more to wish for.
You were the final petal.

CHAPTER TWO

SHOCK

The moment
you viewed me
as something
outside of you,
we were
no longer
one.

I study
the problems posed
by that stuff
surrounding
all of your bones.

He fixed
her damaged wings
with love and compliments,
just to watch her fly
into the arms
of another.

Sometimes Cupid
fires little arrows
at dried tear ducts.

She shoots with words,
but the exit wounds
make her squeamish.

Even in that moment,
I couldn't help
but notice
there were only
those vanishing moments.

The unrepeatable arrangement
of her hair,
the exclusive position
of her body,
they would never
be the same.

The tragedy is not
what we became
but what we could
have been.

Those moments have faded
into my aging skin.

She left.

Taking nothing
but my sleep
and my appetite.

Now I cling
to my sanity.

She is magic.

And in her final trick,
the relationship vanished.

CHAPTER THREE

ANGER

Sitting in silence
as the panic sets in.

Nothing is louder
than the absence
of her presence.

I hear the rising
internal war.

Heartbreak
has shattered
the world
as I know it.

Its foundation
is crumbling.

I vow to warn
the others.

The love
was ripped
from my life
too early.

Pardon me
if these words
taste bitter.

She flew away in a hurry,
leaving only this feather,
with which I now write.

I despise
the gap
between us.

The farther
you are,
the more
I hate
the world.

It wasn't time or distance
that drove us apart.

It was the way the moon
lit the reflection of your body
for my unknown counterpart.

As I prayed for your return,
you were folded
with your knees bent
to meet another's needs.

The antennas on my head
channeled hope.

Yours were gripped
and pulled while you moaned.

She blew the candle out,
and it's been dark ever since.

Left me frozen on the steps
of our engagement.

With a mind already shattered,
she presented me the heart to match.

I'm beautifully asphyxiated
by the lump left in my throat.

Perhaps I looked for depth
within her shallow soul.

It's rather cold in this inferno.
I rub a pen against
a page like kindling
in hopes of burning
every trace of her
within me.

Not sure how
I ever saw
any sort of light
staring into
those black holes
in the center
of your eyes.

Sleep
is the first casualty
during the war on love.

When I close my eyes,
the enemy surrounds me.

The nightmares
she would console me from
were nothing compared to when
she made them a reality.

She chiseled the cold
around my heart,
but the ice pick slipped
and went straight through my chest.

As I melt into a void,
I remain paralyzed
by her moonshine
like a man who catatonically stares
into Medusa's eyes.

I hear the howls of the wolves
begging for her attention
as she makes her selection.

Maybe the scent
of the blood I trail
attracted her,
enamored by the wounds
of my convictions.

As her deceptive mask is unveiled,
I shiver with rage.
I let the devil in,
and she refuses to go away.

I cannot wait for the day
when she is nothing more
than a memory
of the mistakes I've made.

You must be
my eternal damnation.

The only part of me
that burns forever.

I watched her
let him bleed out slowly,
her eyes glossed over,
her shoulders weightless.

He didn't deserve
the pain he endured,
but it was written in stone
before they ever crossed paths.

He tried to grasp
something that eternally
never existed.

I held her claws
and felt the warmth
he once believed
would outlive time.

We walked together
as empathic realization
struck me like lightning.

The cycle of the moon
cannot be stopped by one.

My mouth watered.
It was my turn to drink
from this fountain of life.

I tried to convince myself that
I'd have a different fate.

I saw the others' souls
screaming in agony
as I looked into her eyes.
Peasants who tried to attain
what's only suitable for a king.

I smiled back
and saw
the poor bastard
I would soon become.

Bleeding hearts
eventually bleed out.

Now I write with
the blackest of ink.

Often wonder
if you've seen the red
in the lake of souls
you devoured.

A one hundred-pound goddess
with hypnotic eyes
and the mouth
of a praying mantis.

I became entranced
by the shine of your
deadly ambivalence.

Left my dignity at the door
and entered begging
for scraps of affection
at your feet.

Smile pretty for me, baby.
I still see the shreds
of my heart between your teeth.

The very same
nature must
have designed
the Venus flytrap.

The way that
beautiful smile
opens up
and swallows
a soul whole.

I studied her every angle
with careful precision.

I still can't figure out
where that monster
was hidden.

She conquered me
and set me free
with a flap
over my empty chest.

Evoked the bittersweet life
from my hibernating soul
then drained its essence.

She dominates kingdoms
just to raid their valuables
and moves on to the next.

Her weapons pierce any armor,
and her yoni is nothing more
than a sheath.

She watches the madness
rise in their eyes
and uses the element of surprise
as the theme of her exit.

What a beautiful death wish.

And along her path
of moving on,
a footprint
stains my chest.

I couldn't photograph
the way you left
my insides,
so I painted them
with jagged letters.

They approach
with concerned faces.

You smeared blood
on the aesthetics.

Time doesn't heal all wounds.
It hardens them under a thicker layer of skin
for someone else to uncover.

Solitude became
the only option.

I wear the stain
of you on my
expressions.

Sitting in a small room
with the walls closing in,
I open my chest
and let the rapture begin.

The mind is connected to a rat feeder,
addicted to epinephrine,
and I lack the receptors
for acceptance.

Looking for substance
in a field of knuckle-dragging peasants
with limited imaginations.

Their souls lack presence,
an entire species
that functions solely
for stimulation.

Thought I had found
a true goddess, friendship,
and a spiritual companion.

Turns out
she was only focused
on the appendage
attached to my lower abdomen.

My apologies . . .
I had you confused
with someone I'd be buried next to.

The grass
only looks greener
because you haven't
trampled on it yet.

Another weekend night,
and I'm high on ink fumes.

You're down at the watering hole
where they take shots
of artificial happiness
from the empty hole
in your chest.

Crocodile smiles rub fingertips
along the skin of your bones
and only pause
when they reach for joints.

You stick a tap
in the wet bag
on my sleeve
and wring it dry
with every drink.

I may be an unwilling member
of the bleeding hearts club,
but you step into clubs
and become a bar slut.

Stop searching
for deep roots
in potted plants.

Shallowness
is only meant
for short-lived
interactions.

Most live a superficial life
consumed by what they look like,
but they only attract flies
because they're rotting
on the inside.

There is no rest for the wicked,
but I refuse to sleep with the fickle.

Some feel life more than most alive.
There is an art in finding the delicate composure
to carefully describe chaotic dysfunction.
One I seek to master before writing the ending.
I would rather paint pain on a page
than decorate a wall with gray and white matter.
Until I choose the latter,
don't ask about my condition.
The disorders are vast,
like the depth of the tunnel
I choose to live in.

Perhaps we are more than wage slaves in meat cages,
perseverating about the little free time we get
from begging for scraps at a table
we're not welcome
to sit at.

They smile. And all I see is cutlery.

My self-hatred derives
from the realization
that I'm one of you.

My spine collapses
under the weight of a faked interest
in what you say.

It's hard to take a compliment
when you're repulsed
by your own reflection.

They told me the best way
to kill the devil is to face him,
so I cut everyone off
and have stared in the mirror
every day since.

The mind can be
a dangerous place,
and mine is set
to self-detonate.

Your positive thoughts
don't resonate,
and I'm content to lie
to your face.

Until I sterilize myself
of these bacteria,
I remain disgusted
with this petri dish.

I watch you rub
your dirty hands
on the same napkin
you clean your mouth with.

Your orifice
smiles with
no regret.

Stay away
from me.

I can smell
the death
on your breath.

Throw a gem
into a hollow head
and hear it echo
with emptiness.

Pierce a chest
full of innocence
and watch it ooze
sorrow.

I have witnessed
immortal souls
cling to dogmatic
elements of love
and be carried
to an early death.

Do not trust
the tears in the eyes
of those with fangs
dripping with passion
from the lives
they've absorbed.

Chapter Four

Bargaining

He sees the skeleton
inside the beauty
that she hides behind.

The core of her being
forever shines like
pale moonlight.

Pheromones seep
through walls of
distant memories
and replenish
the presence of all
that is empty.

Hunched over
a missing rib,
unable to walk
with his spine
upright,
he travels far from home
with feet of stone.

A fist of bones still holds
a flower that has
turned to mulch.

No matter
the strength
of my grip,
time keeps
replacing
your hand.

And when I
looked for beauty
in another place,
I kept seeing
your face.

I could never love someone else
because someone else
will always be
someone else.

I never had an option
when it came to loyalty.

Even when they tried
to steal that piece of me,
my love became obsolete.

I would rid you
from my desires,
but I would have
none left.

You remain
the missing half
of my empty glass.

He was callous
to the mistakes he made,
but there was something about
those liquid spears that left her face.

The day your smile vanished.

It was gone before you left,
a victim of my self-loathing
and manic depression.

I lost my sense of direction.

I wandered countless days
but only found you
when I'd cry myself
into a dream—

A look of clarity
sits in your eyes,
and it opens
my chest entirely.

No resentment.
No distrust.
No reservation.

Just frozen moments of perfection.

Despite all that's been said,
your first language was love.

It feels like only
those soft lips
could cushion
my fall.

I miss how you
teach me about me.

You are the point of reference
for my relationship
with the opposite sex.
My Juliette.

Only treated you less
because I envy
the power you hold
over my mind's ability to rest.

I crave your estrogen
and elegant dialect.

I walked the steps
of a childhood
filled with neglect
and came home
to find you had left.

Looking at the creases
of the empty spot
on this bed,
I'm reminded
that I'll never forget.

Your final lesson
has taught me regret.

A broken heart
would shatter
a million times over
just to feel once more
what made it whole.

This knot in my neck
reminds me to keep
my head straight.

Perhaps these discomforts
teach us better ways
to navigate
treacherous landscapes.

They say I've become distant,
but I don't know what that means
I've never been close to anybody.

No time for enemies.
I'm diagnosed with PTSD
because of the things
I've seen in my sleep.

The pen became my best friend
and the words accompanied.

She tried to show me
what it's like to feel happy,
but I couldn't find a new identity.

She gave me her body
like it was the part of the dish
she didn't want.
I was full from the last helping.
I only wanted her heart.

The mental midgets
and moral maggots
manipulate her
out of her dress,
but I was only looking
for my rightful place
on the left side of her chest.

I have witnessed
many cycles of the moon,
but this one has shifted my direction.

Perhaps I've been selfish
and need to accept that she
must grace other worlds
with her presence.

It's difficult to remain
in the moment when
I know her intentions.

My moods turn
to tides that crash
into the little time we have left.
I can only focus
on the times she has left.

Those dark spots
must be what she's like
underneath.
She says I'm dramatic.
I say she speaks
in redundancies.

My mind is in the clouds,
and I'm trying to pull
the monogamy
out of her astrology.
This is the plight
of codependency.

Sometimes I think about
leaving this celestial body
by splattering my stardust
inside the pyramid lobby.

Maybe then
she would remember me,
and we'd live happily
inside a permanent dream.

I need to calm down, breathe,
and remind myself that tomorrow
will bring another evening.

I have ruined
our once-in-a-lifetime.

Pardon if I seem eager
to reach the next.

I'd rather keep you
in my dreams.

It's the only place
I find the missing piece
that makes us complete.

Somewhere out there,
perhaps in a parallel universe,
you and I are lovers.
And somehow
that thought
comforts me here.

Lost,
walking for days
through the rain
in pitch black,

even my view
of the moonlight
is covered by clouds.

This was the map
I drew while blinded
by my own self-resentments.

I ignored the spiders
as they whispered clues
about the storm's arrival.

The webs have been built,
and I'm wrapped
in thoughts
of redemption.

It's been a long time
coming—to emerge from
my shortcomings.

And I may be gone for a while,
but I promise to return
a better man with the rising sun.

Forgotten bones
line the walls
of catacombs.

And as I pace
inside the cage
that's placed
behind my face,

I still hear
the whisper
of her soul.

CHAPTER FIVE

DEPRESSION

Depression is the cancer of the soul.
Some inherit it, others develop it;
some put it into remission and others are consumed by it.
The word *disease* cannot describe how your own mind
leaves you to rot in a debilitative cage.

We are death
on vacation.

I've come to realize
the older I get,
and with each
heartbreak,
I lose more
tolerance
for the
sun.

The lines
on my face
have merged
with the cracks
in my chest.

And they all
trace back
to the day
you left.

I no longer smile.
I've lost the muscle strength.

My better half is dead.
Now I drag this bag of flesh.

Sometimes it hurts
just to breathe.

She vanished
into the very air
that I inhale.

Another late night
in my room just pacing,
ruminating
on the various ways
to take a permanent vacation.

Scattered emotions
flow together like
letters in cursive.
I am a mental illness
trapped in a person.

She showed me
what it's like to never exist,
and I wish I never looked.
My spine rests
in the same shape
as an abortion hook.

She left
and I've been living
in a post-apocalyptic
state ever since.

I need to abandon
these thoughts.
Often fantasize
about being homeless
and pushing around
this heavy heart
inside of a shopping cart.

Opportunities were squandered,
and I wonder what it's like
for my children to be growing up
with a depressed father.

Perhaps I should have bought
another letter after my name.
The sound of garbage trucks
in the morning remind me
that it's a new day.

I give myself another mundane cliché
and peel my face off a pillow
to go stand in line at the community slave trade.

Been close to death
more times than
I've been close to life.

It's getting harder
to differentiate
nightmares from reality.

Flapping the stubs
on my self-
amputated wings.

Pardon me,
I've had a little
too much to think.

Experience
symptoms of delirium
during times of writing.

Desperate to translate
emotion into letters
before I vanish.

The sky is beginning to look more like a cage.

The memories
thicken
as you fade into
impermanence.

Pardon my distance.
I've been busy thinking
myself sick,

acknowledging that many
won't hear from me again.
I owe more phone calls
than I have time left.

I'm too selfish to share
these self-resentments,
and I'd rather send
my salutations
through the wind.

Bill said, *Heavy is the head*,
but I'll likely bleed to death
from the thorns instead.

Perhaps it's the karma
of being a sinner.
The slices of happiness
are getting thinner.

I have a knapsack
full of hardship,
and I'm out chasing storms
on a beautiful afternoon.

Even though I'm just
a speck of dirt,
the concentration
inside this little chest
could crack a hole
in the center
of the universe.

I snapped
the puppet strings
behind my face
that plays pretend.

Now look away—
my windows are filling up
with rain again.

She took my treasures
and left me with a sunken chest.

There is a war drum
in her chest.

It beats the tune
of my destruction.

She had consumed
my entire life,
but to her
I remain
nothing more
than bed crumbs.

If only
my reasons
for loving you
were as clear
as the tears
I now look through.

I haven't been outside
since she went away.
I'm no longer fooled
by the looks of a beautiful day.

Not even the deceitful sun
could hold a flame
to the light she once gave.

I live in my own world.

Yours is too cold
and distant.

Take a positive thought,
crumple and toss it into
the wasteland of my mind.

I boiled hope
with a solvent of confidence
and ended up
with concentrated nonsense.

I try to balance
on this ball of stress,
but I remain top-heavy
with this well-guarded head case.

She walked away
as the pathetic smile
slowly vanished from my face.

I recoiled back
into that unsafe place
that no one else can tolerate.

Stuck in the fog of my mind
and I can't tell if I'm all out of steam
or if there's too much Diphenhydramine
running through my blood stream.

I apply pressure to my mind
to find the fault line
of my mistakes.

Our forever ended,
but her soft flesh
has been carved
into my memory bank.

I've exhausted
the different ways
to explain how I'm not okay.

There's something wrong
with my brain,
and I keep losing
bodyweight.

In my mid-thirties,
still dealing with
teenage angst,

I place this body on a stake,
and I'm ashamed to say
I'm in love
with a woman
with a head of snakes.

I go to bed each day
in hopes of leaving
this awful place
and wake to find myself
at my father's wake.

God is a comedian—
the loop button
is the only one that plays.

There is no escape.
You only spawn
into another piece
of biodegradable waste.

I become more fatigued
with each second I breathe.
My mind is trapped
in the space between you and me.

I look for distractions,
but I fail to forget
how they're all happy,
and all I can think
of is how my tax dollars
contribute to death.

I've lost count
of how many nights
I couldn't sleep
and the many more times
I hit snooze.
I only write
to keep my hands
from tying a noose.

I try to gather some peace,
but I'm awakened
by those collecting
the debts that I've left.

So I deteriorate my liver
with what I use
to turn off my head.

It's hard to get out of bed
and dress
when you're comfortably
depressed.

We have vastly different
definitions of success.
I'm only looking
for a decent night's rest.

Stuck in a cell,
this planet is eating itself
and defecating humans.

And I don't want
to talk to them.
I traded friends
for paper and a pen.

I died at the thought
of you with other men.
Now I write to bury
this exposed skeleton.

She wants to know
what she already knew.
Tell her that I'm back,
used, and unimproved.

Since the day
I was pulled
from the incubator,
I've been familiar
with those who
become strangers.

Obsessed with these
depressed thoughts.
Step into the mind
of a man filled
with the ever-growing
presence of loss.

I'm aware it's disturbing.
If you see me in passing,
please don't disturb me.
I'm in a hurry to go do nothing.

Sometimes art imitates death.
It isn't me
who moves this pen—
the Earth is suicidal.

I take a bow
as I descend
into a downward spiral.

Sitting on a park bench
staring inward.

I see the growing mountains
of sadness in the past
and the abyss of darkness
on the horizon.

The sound of children's laughter
echoes through the abandoned valleys
and quickly dissipates
into the fog.

I stand on both knees
and feel the roots beneath me
reaching to consume
this aging shell.

These inner workings
of karmic hell
trap me in a cycle
of birth and death,
a tired, restless soul
that can only wish
to feel less.

And I still see her
through my inability
to look in a mirror.

That old, dead moon
continues to collect
new compliments.

The earth is so
self-absorbed
it bleeds water
onto itself.

Meanwhile,
the sun just waits
to burn it all.

Be careful how wide you open your arms for someone.
You run the risk of bleeding out.

Be careful with love.
That stuff is highly flammable.

Come here . . .
let me show you
why the last one left.

I selfishly set fire
to every relationship
and used the ashes as ink
to write about the way it burns.

The sustenance of inspiration
is sickening.
Been dry drinking so long,
I'm drunk on dehydration.

A captain of a ship
that sets sail into horizons
which swallow moons whole.

The future holds
cigarette butts
floating in bed pans
and a grumpy old man
who writes of his past.

Forgive me if I seem distracted.
My thoughts are louder
than the sounds you make
from that hole on your face.

Don't stand too close.
Plastic love melts next
to eternal hell fire.

I don't battle with depression.
I go to bed with it.

She wishes me sweet dreams.
If only she knew
wishes don't mean a thing.

You can throw handfuls
of pennies into this well,
but it's bottomless.

Demons guard the steps
of my attempts to rest.

The angel
that would take my hand
and guide me safely to sleep
now waits on the other side
to tear me piece by piece.

And I would die
to feel that bliss again,
to incubate within
a womb of peacefulness,
where mom protects me
from these evil women.

Trapped
in a self-impending doom.

Remembering the sky
that once opened
and wrapped her loving arms
around my gloom.

A connection like sun rays
that make flowers bloom.

It took the dead of night
to show those days are through.

I've said goodbye to many words,
and they don't come
as easily as they used to.

How long have I been chasing you?

My last body was consumed.
I cracked out of a new cocoon
and continued flying towards the moon.

They say the good die young,
and I've already outlived Jesus.

My heart is shattered.
Perhaps that's what she meant
when she said she'd love me to pieces.

I gave up on
the pursuit of happiness
because that stuff doesn't exist.

Told one too many tales of my demise.
Perhaps I should explore the afterlife.

The devil's in disguise,
inside the one I'd call a wife.

Death is nothing but a word for fate.

She remains the face of all my blame,
and I don't even remember her name.

It all started
with a glance
at pretty faces.

Now my heart
is smashed
between
these pages.

I don't have much,
but I carry my bags
beneath my eyes.

Here you are again,
stuck in my neural pathways.

This inability to function
is paving my way to an early grave.

Woke up inside a skeleton prison.
I lack optimism,

and the way I've been living
is starting to change
my physical composition.

It's difficult to erase
the thoughts in the memory bank
when you're caged in
a place that sits behind your face.

Instead of accepting any personal blame,
I point back at you and
anthropomorphize the pain.

Every night I black my thoughts out
facedown in a pillow.

Awakening each day
into the nightmare
left by those I've slept beside.

Here I am,
alive and unwell,
unsoundly sleeping
in the bed I made.

Home is the place
you reside in
most often,
and this room
has become a coffin.

Love was all
I ever wanted,
so I strangled myself
with the invisible cord
that keeps the universe
from collapsing.

Hope is a fickle bitch,
and cynicism
is her bastard son.

Inadequacy
continually speaks
from my reflection.

This spherical pattern
of endings never stops,
and I'm suspended
in mid-death.

They offer life,
and I continue to walk away,
feeling like a dog
with his tail between his legs,

aware that I need
to fix my head
before I decide
to drag myself
behind the shed.

I have tried happiness.
That stuff is highly unstable.

Smiling too much will hurt your face.

I can force
my face to bend
in many ways,
but a smile
never matches
my eyes.

They express concern
for my well-being.
They say the stress
will murder me,
but I've been living
this way for an eternity.

Don't worry,
I haven't yet found
the method of my escape.
I'm still looking
for different ways
to purge the pain.

One day
I'll only exist
in the æther.

Don't take it personally.
I'm not responding
to anyone else either.

Some misery hates company,
so what do you want from me?

I escape from others
with a sense of urgency.

I have scores to settle
with forces greater.

I'll talk to you later.
I'm playing a game of chicken
with my creator.

It's adorable
the way we
cradle pain
and nurse it
into a life
of its own.

Pain
has brought me here
to tell me its story.

Face down
with a handful of grey hair,
I find the allegory—
new experiences still use
the same old mechanism to feel.
All of our passions become dull.

I have nothing
but these thoughts.

Words traced
around the splatter
of tear drops.

The insides are a mess.

This isn't art:
It's coagulated chunks
from a rotting heart.

Discharge
leaks from depression,
a lesion
that's sore to the touch
like an infection.

Won't stand to speak
with other faces.
And if I tell them
it's too dark to walk,
they'll take away my shoelaces.

Everything
happening around me
is secondary.

Don't mind me,
I'm in a continuous
session of therapy.

A manic depressive
who daily stretches
the limits of polarity.

I can move these limbs,
but I can't control
what's happening within.

The cracks
in this heart
have become my
individual fingerprints.

The identity
of having no identity
is still better than
what most pretend to be.

I'm down to the last belt loop,
and it's too late
to trade in these shoes.

Emaciated
but my hunger pangs
for something
beyond food.

A voodoo doll
covered with
puncture wounds,

I stab myself
in the gut with this pen
and watch the pain
spill onto this page.

I write my "Dear Jane" prison letters
from a skull-sized cage.

The sustenance
of what used to be life
has become oversaturated and stale.

The embryonic clones
are mass-produced
and ghost-less.

Adult babies
rebel against parents
that were never there.

I can feel your pain, child.

The more you cry for help,
the less dressed you become.

Wish I could nourish
that empty space.

Tumultuous ignorance only drowns
the breath of what needs to be embraced.

I see loneliness
in that smile
you show others.

There is a quiet place
where we all gather alone.

I'll meet you there.

Disoriented
from walking in circles
with a broken compass.

This mechanism
for measuring love
has led me in the
wrong direction.

I'm homelessly romantic.

A veteran of internal war
who panhandles for hope.

Just thought you should know
that thing you threw in the trash
grew mold, crawled out,
and found its way into a poem.

Keep your
simple happiness.

There is much more
depth in darkness.

With dull eyes,
life begins to grow
from the cracks of my fingertips.

It was only when I looked inside
that I found what I coveted.

This skull is rusted
from the tears
that fall out of its holes.

The weight
of scattered memories
often makes this
cage of bone float.

I drift past the present
into the unknown,
feet split open from
walking on the shards
of a broken home.

My soul seeps out of a pen hole.

Sitting in a bathtub,
focused on letting
my blood flow back
into the ocean.

Our boat was swallowed
by the horizon before
I ever noticed.

I ran my fingers across
the future of my own pain.
As long as she was here,
the world had a name.

I have felt the texture
of heaven and hell.
If only I could have known
what was under that shell.

The mood is blue,
but he smiles
with yellow teeth.

He masquerades
the devastation
with a look of apathy.

This isn't a cry for sympathy:
That small violin
already plays his symphony.

The mask no longer fits
around his weathered face.
Every day it morphs
into someone
that disappointed him
yesterday.

Open wounds bleed
through the gauze
of human interaction.

Stagnated melancholy
is desperate for his subtraction.

Ambiguous about ambition
because his alma mater
is this condition.

Sometimes potential
wilts before it blossoms.

The complexion of grey
slowly covering his face
is clear evidence that he
is fading away.

Perhaps it was all for the better.

He now looks to solidify
a slice of immortality
through an arrangement of letters.

Poetry is alive,
but all the true poets have died.

They sailed from stagnant waters
to stare at a beauty
the ocean doesn't recognize.

They no longer
share the same argon
with this ossified body of life.

The clandestine whispers
of the wind have been ignored.
The rain no longer shares
its stories with the bored.

Meaning continues to fall
from the earth like the leaves
of aging trees.

The seed of the future
gives birth to the empty.

I often wonder why
I feel so dead inside,
but then I remember that all
the true poets have died.

I have traveled lifetimes
to sit in this unpleasant
moment,

worlds apart
from where I am
and where I thought
I was going.

At least the word hope
is in hopeless.

I get flashbacks of feeling from colors
that existed before everything turned grey.

I see glimpses of light bouncing reflections
from puddles between the pauses of rain.

I cheat death
by finding epiphanies
that mean more than life.

If only I could be there for extended
periods of time.

To sneak past the doors
we're kept behind
and peer into the dreary eyes
of the divine.

Existentialism
holds my interest
while I'm condemned to
this existence.

I have passed the darkness
of wanting to turn off
the light switch.

I only care
to meet with God
to settle our differences.

Pardon me,
you weren't
supposed
to see that.

Sometimes
the trauma is
in between masks.

Only paper can hold
the weight of some words.

They said my writing
was one of a kind,
so I presented the world
with the fragmented pieces
of a broken mind.

The true answers never
came from blending in.
I remove cancer
with surgical penmanship.

You can't know life
through the words
of other men;
the signs of the times
are felt through the wind.

All their morals sound monotone,
and I never learned their language.
I'm at home, depressed
and full of anguish.

And I remain confused:
She walked out the room
with my sanity glued
to the bottom of her shoe.

Famished,
but I keep digesting
the words that she used.

Hate spewed
from the only lips
I ever wanted to kiss.

Since then I've tried to hide
behind broken eyelids.

Those unwell wishes
you threw in the well
worked well.
Now I am left with this story to tell.

How could I
ever forget
when the moon
is attributed
solely to you.

Things haven't
been the same
since I was forced
to say goodbye.

Now I stand
in the rain
to feel a piece
of the sky.

She is learning the ropes,
keeping an assortment of souls
inside of a glass case.
Broken hearts are her collection.

Each one represents a subtle growth
in the building blocks
of her desensitization.

Her body armor
consists of a soft flesh
that creates further distance
from those she presses it against.

Soon enough
she'll join the sea of survivalists
who have abandoned the pure
meaning of a kiss.

She shares her flesh
but doesn't dare
to make eye contact.

To show the vulnerability
of what she hides inside
poses too much danger.

Just another exchange
of bodily fluids with
a complete stranger.

I see the spots
on the moon like
bruises on her thighs,
enjoyed by those who
continue to multiply.

She's always been curled
in the fetal position,
mentally beaten
into a state of submission.

Pain becomes joy
when it doesn't have an ending.
I can hear the trapped bird
in her chest plate singing.

It's not just a bedroom:
It's a sanctuary.

It's not just flesh:
It's divinity.

If only she could see
the sanctity
in the parts of herself
she gives away so easily.

As life begins to vanish
with each passing breath,
I write about loss
because it's all I have left.

These empty hands
grasp for a past
that's filled with regret.

So absent now
that I'm becoming
just like the father
I never met.

Letters touch nerve endings
that stem from the lump
in his throat.

It is he who wrings tears
into beautiful poems.

I'm determined
to find the value
of a human life.

To unearth
what it takes
to put another
under earth.

The final push
that causes a tear
to leap from its eyelid.

That hesitation
before the pull of a trigger
must be measured
before I leave here.

The reconciliation
of a mind before
it divorces itself
from a spine.

The strength of the thread
one clings to before
wrapping it around a neck.

Let's encapsulate
this feeling
and pass it to those
who need healing.

Let us find the pearl
in the peril of this planet.

I can feel the urgency of time
in this little frame of mine,
and I'd die to plant a thorn
of guilt in the divine.
Let us hang the one
who sits in heaven
just to put us through this hell.
This is a call to all,
but then I realize
they're too busy watching football.

In a society frozen with insecurity, the inability to express emotion causes insanity. Those who do express emotion are labeled as weak. In fact, this inability to emote is the main symptom of schizophrenia. One cannot suppress emotion without negative consequences. Words alone cannot describe (that) which yearns for liberation. This is why art is vital to our well-being.

CHAPTER SIX

ACCEPTANCE

True love encompasses the entire spectrum of human emotion.
It may travel to the depths of hatred,
but it always returns home.

You can try to pull her wings off,
but her heart will fly away.

I grabbed a handful
of your love but left
empty-handed.

I swam through
an ocean of serpents
to live inside
the darkness
of your eyes.

Devastation hit
my troubled mind.

And I've yet
to make it out
the other side.

But you no longer
get to tell me
how to die.

It was in
this lifetime
that I'd never
see you again.

I would have
tried once more,
but the stars
were broken.

Maybe lost love
was meant to be lost.
Sometimes a memory
is more beautiful
than the present.

All skeletons
appear to smile.

Perhaps some
memories
never
die.

You remain
the white haze
that keeps me up at night.

My eyelids won't shut right;
the tears have
crystallized.

Sleeping pills
become obsolete
when each breath
awakens the agony.

Still wondering
where you went,
but all the questions have left.

Slowly churning thoughts
of how quickly you
moved onto the next.

I'm exhausted
from wrestling with bed sheets.

Up since the sun set
when it finally dawns on me:
I didn't lose love,
I lost sleep.

I found art
as you untwined
from me,

as I watched dead leaves
have their final dance
as they fell from a tree.

And I wrote
until the black
ran out . . .

For as bad as it is,
it's not as bad
as it seems,
staring at
a mirror,
talking
to the
enemy.

They didn't take my self-confidence:
I gave it away.
They didn't lower my self-esteem:
I never had any.
They didn't break my spirit:
It was never whole.
I wasn't dependent on them:
I lacked independence.
I wasn't trapped in pain:
I refused to embrace it.
I didn't gain this realization:
I only tried to erase it.

All that anyone
can ever truly give you
is a feeling, a feeling
that you already own.

Every tear shed is a drop of pure freedom.
Each brings you closer to ending what causes the pain.
Embrace the burdens you carry:
They strengthen the legs along the path to liberation.

The rain comes from the very same place we endlessly chase.

Find the beauty
in your pain.

That moisture
on your eyes
is what makes
them glimmer.

Let the tears
cascade down
through your cemented feet.

You can then
move forward.

Don't forget how far you've come,
even if where you are
isn't where you'd like to be.

Look how much you've achieved
with a life you never asked
to receive.

I know how low you felt
when the pain pulsed
with every heartbeat,
alone in your home,
trembling with agony.

Tears taste like salt
rubbed into wounds,
completely consumed
with incessant depression.

I am a product of that plight:

Those days when
you hate the birds
as they chirp reminders
to get up and deal with your life.

Those moments when
your only hope
is to be embraced
by a rope around your throat.

To levitate
one last time
above the earth
until flailing limbs go limp
and dance with the wind
as you become one
with the body of the universe.

It's hard to see past the hurt
when all you can do
is stare in reverse.

For what it's worth,
you're not an introvert:
You're a diamond surrounded by dirt.

Sometimes solitude
is the worst place to hide in.

The only way I survived
was to learn to love life
as much as I despise it.

When life tries to kill you,
the best revenge
is to remain alive.

The hardest part
was accepting
that I'd be
okay.

You are a display of art
as you open and unfold.
I hope you reach
the full extent of your bloom
and present the magnificence
of your grace to this earth
before its elements
wilt and drop you
back into the dirt.

If only we could see our endings
as beautiful as autumn leaves.

Life is short,
and every kiss
is numbered.

But so is every tear.

Only love
should disrupt
the peace
of solitude.

If you must choose
something to be good at,
let it be love.

The rest will follow.

I knew:
I had found love,
when in the end
all that remained
was poetry.

Acknowledgements

These cleverly self-deprecating, mediocre poems were largely inspired, encouraged, or provoked by the magnificence of the following individuals: Her (A.P., M.C., S.J., D.S., J.R., V.D., J.H., and A.V.); my children, Vincent and Marley; my beautiful mother and grandmother; my brothers, David and Matt, and my sister, Sofia; my best friend, Phil Rees; my therapists and mentors, Sean O'Hara, Dwayne Bradford, Rabb Love, Rebecca Williams, and Melissa Tralla. Also, Iz Balleto, Melissa Hammett, Thomas "Atma" Stewart, Ben "SoS" Johnson, Ben Stewart, Lydia Leyva, Garrison Doreck, April Doyle, Roxy Walnum, Scott Tuttle, and Michelle "Ghost" Martin. Artists Joshua "Cubbiebear" Bailey, Paul "Sage" Francis, Sean "Slug" Daley, Jonathan "Maulskull" Messinger, Douglas "Emancipator" Appling, Israel "Nash" Gripka, Cody "Sadistik" Foster, Saul Williams, and Beck for his album *Sea Change*. Special thanks to Kallie Falandays for polishing this turd.

Don Solt and Richard Cerutti: Even in my darkest days, you remained present in a sunbeam. Thank you for everything.

Made in the USA
Monee, IL
27 December 2020

55708532R00122